JN274177

English in 30 Seconds

Award-Winning TV Commercials from Cannes Lions

［カンヌ国際広告祭受賞］
ＴＶコマーシャルで学ぶ異文化の世界

Masayuki Aoki

NAN'UN-DO

English in 30 Seconds
Award-Winning TV Commercials from Cannes Lions

Copyright© 2009

Masayuki Aoki

All Rights Reserved

No part of this book may be reproduced in any form without written permission from the author and Nan'un-do Co., Ltd.

TV Commercials: Copyright ©2000, 2001, 2002, 2003, 2004, 2005
Cannes International Advertising Festival, Ltd.
Toei Agency—Official Festival Representative of Cannes Lions

映像協力
カンヌ国際広告祭日本代表
株式会社東映エージエンシー

TO THE STUDENT

The TV commercials featured in this textbook are the best of the best. They were all award winners at the world's biggest TV advertisement festival held in Cannes, France, every summer. They are compact, well designed, skillfully shot, often humorous, and full of up-to-date colloquial English expressions. At the same time, they deal with important social activities, cultural phenomena, and contemporary themes. Thus, studying these commercials will not only improve your English listening and speaking skills, but it will also contribute to your intercultural education and expand your knowledge in general. And you'll have a good time doing it, too.

The innovative learning strategies used in this book take full advantage of everything these wonderful commercials have to offer. All the exercises were designed to help you better understand natural-speed spoken English and to build up your stock of useful English words and phrases. The activities also give you the opportunity to become a "storyteller" by reproducing the commercials' story lines in English and even to "act" as the "stars" of the commercials. The following is a brief explanation of the various sections and activities that make up each unit.

Tasks for the Preliminary Reading

● *Preliminary Reading*

The preliminary reading of each unit is an article of about 300 words that provides essential background information and ideas related to the commercial(s) for each unit.

● *Vocabulary Build-up*

This exercise asks you to match key words highlighted in the preliminary reading with the appropriate synonyms, descriptions, or definitions.

● *Reading Comprehension*

In this task, you must choose the one sentence out of four that most closely matches the main ideas and information of the reading passage.

Tasks for the TV Commercials

● *Vocabulary Preview*

This word warm-up activity introduces you to key words/phrases used in the commercial(s) by asking you to match them with words/phrases of similar meaning.

● *Soundtrack Listening*

In this task, you first listen to the soundtrack of the commercial(s) without looking at the screen. You must then number the words/phrases/sentences listed in your text in the order in which they are heard in the commercial.

● *Story Line Completion/Scene Description*

For this activity, after you watch a commercial, you must complete its story line by putting sentences describing the commercial's scenes in the order in which they appear. In some units, you are asked to write short-sentence answers to questions about the commercial(s).

● *Transcript Completion*

Here, you must fill in blanks in transcripts of the commercial(s) as you listen to and watch the commercial(s) again. In some units, you must put words/phrases into the correct order to make sentences from the commercial(s).

● *Finding the Commercial's Message*

Some units ask you to choose the one sentence out of three that best expresses the main message of the commercial(s).

● *Utilizing Useful Words and Phrases*

Here, you must make sentences utilizing key words/phrases either by translating sentences from Japanese to English or putting words/phrases in the correct order.

● *Optional Activity*

In this activity, you "act" out the scenes in the commercial(s) by reading or reciting your completed transcripts as you watch the commercial(s) with the sound off.

● *Topics for Discussion*

This last section offers three or four discussion questions based on themes suggested by the commercial(s). You can either discuss the questions in class directly or write out brief answers before you enter discussions.

USING THE DVD

The DVD's main menu consists of 15 unit icons. Click on the unit you want and the sub-menu will appear. Use the sub-menu as follows:

Audio-Video Combination	Commercial appears with both sound and picture. Use for the "Story Line Completion" and "Finding the Commercial's Message" activities.
Audio Only	Commercial's soundtrack only. Use for "Soundtrack Listening" and "Transcription Completion."
Video Only	Commercial appears without sound. Use for "Optional Activity."
Preliminary Reading	Audio recording of the unit's "Preliminary Reading" article.

CONTENTS

Unit 1	Meijer—Higher Standards, Lower Prices	6
Unit 2	This Calls for a Bud Light	11
Unit 3	Anti-Discrimination Campaign	16
Unit 4	McDonald's—King of Fast-Food Restaurants	20
Unit 5	Relax, it's FedEx.	25
Unit 6	BMW—A Car beyond Reason	29
Unit 7	Banking for the Filthy Rich	33
Unit 8	Learning Languages	38
Unit 9	Pepsi—Ask for More	42
Unit 10	United Nations Development Programme	47
Unit 11	Disney—Magic Happens	52
Unit 12	Coca-Cola—For Everyone	57
Unit 13	Anti-Smoking Campaign	61
Unit 14	Counterfeit Mini Coopers	65
Unit 15	Hallmark of a Teacher	69

Unit 1

Meijer—Higher Standards, Lower Prices

I. Preliminary Reading:
This section provides preliminary background information for the TV commercials you are going to watch and listen to. Read the passage carefully and do the tasks that follow.

©2004 MEIJER-Boyfriend (Bronze Lion)

　　The supermarket is considered to be one of America's most effective innovations because it has dramatically changed the lives of people in many countries. The most important characteristics of the supermarket are its self-service system and massive displays of a wide variety of merchandise sold at reasonable prices. Michael Kullen,
5 later known as King Kullen, opened his first self-service supermarket in Queens, New York City, in 1930, realizing his dream of creating mass merchandising and high-volume sales at low profit margins. During the Great Depression of the 1930s, supermarkets boomed and spread all over the United States.
　　The growing popularity of the automobile helped spur the supermarket boom.
10 Supermarkets' large parking lots allowed customers to buy food in bulk for the coming week and bring it home in their cars. Today, American-style supermarkets are found around the world. Some are now so large that they are called hypermarkets or mega-markets and deal in almost all the goods and services that exist in the world of commerce: meat, dairy products, produce, seafood, flowers, clothing, books, computers and
15 software, home electronics, jewelry, and furniture. Many even have tire shops, pharmacies, hearing aid centers, optometrists, and gas stations.
　　Many customers are fascinated and overwhelmed by the products and services available and are often persuaded to buy even more than they had intended to. Some customers, however, criticize supermarkets and hypermarkets because they tend to
20 turn people into shopaholics who are addicted to buying much more than they actually need and who are never completely happy or satisfied no matter how much they buy. Shopping can be fun, but careful planning should come first.

2. Vocabulary Build-up: *Find the* highlighted *words in the reading that match the following descriptions and write them in the parentheses, as in the example.*

Example: To judge or complain about (*criticize*)
1. Milk, butter, and cheese ( )
2. Goods presented for sale ( )
3. The money gained from business ( )
4. A specialist in examining the eyes ( )
5. A motorcar for drivers and passengers ( )

3. Reading Comprehension: *Choose the sentence below which most closely matches the content of the reading passage.*

1. Customers began buying food in bulk for the coming week when cars became popular all over the U.S. in the 1930s.
2. King Kullen opened his first supermarket in New York City in 1930, and later his mass merchandising system spread across the United States and around the world.
3. Some supermarkets are called mega-markets because they don't have tire shops, gas stations, or hearing aid centers.
4. Supermarkets make large profits because they turn their customers into shopping addicts who buy more than they actually need.

Tasks for TV Commercials No. 1 and No. 2

4. Vocabulary Preview: *Here are some key words/phrases you need to know to understand the TV commercials for this lesson. Match each with a word/phrase of similar meaning in the box below.*

1. spinach ( )   2. brand ( )   3. take a bite ( )
4. sweetie ( )   5. bring someone by ( )

```
a. trademark    b. beloved person    c. a kind of vegetable    d. invite    e. try
```

5. Soundtrack Listening: *Listen to the soundtrack of TV Commercial No. 2 without looking at the screen. Then number the words/phrases/sentences below in the order in which you hear them. You can replay the soundtrack as many times as you like. Two have been done for you as examples.*

a. Sweetie (1)   e. Really nice ( )
b. The one ( )   f. See you later. (6)
c. My boyfriend Spider ( )   g. Shopping to do ( )
d. Tonight ( )   h. Angel ( )

6. Story Line Completion: *The sentences below describe the scenes in the commercials for this lesson. Watch the video and then complete the commercials' story lines by numbering the sentences in the order in which the scenes appear, as in the examples.*

TV Commercial No. 1

1. The girl does not like the spinach. ( )
2. There is a girl sitting at a table and a man standing beside her. (1)
3. The man gives the girl a taste of the MEIJER brand spinach. ( )
4. The girl does not like this spinach, either. ( )
5. The man asks the girl to try the national brand spinach. ( )

TV Commercial No. 2

1. A girl and a tall, rugged-looking young man are shopping in a supermarket. (1)
2. The boyfriend ignores his girlfriend's father. ( )
3. The parents seem pleased with their daughter's boyfriend. ( )
4. The father tries to shake hands with his daughter's boyfriend. ( )
5. The girl's parents run into her and the young man. ( )
6. The girl introduces her boyfriend to her parents. ( )
7. The father invites his daughter's boyfriend to dinner. ( )

7. Transcript Completion: *As you watch and listen to the commercials again, fill in the blanks in the transcripts below.*

TV Commercial No. 1

Tester:	OK, Abby, _____ the national _____.
Girl:	Ugh . . .
Tester:	Good. _____ the MEIJER _____.
Girl:	Ugh . . .
Tester:	Good.

TV Commercial No. 2

Mom:	Hey, _____.
Daughter:	_____, _____.
Dad:	Hi, Angel. _____?
Daughter:	This is my boyfriend Spider.
Dad:	Oh, hi, Spider. _____.
	Well, we've _____.
	But _____?
Daughter:	OK.
Mom:	We'll _____ then.
	Oh, _____.
Dad:	Yeah, _____.

8. Finding the Commercial's Message: *Choose the sentence that best expresses the main message of each commercial.*

TV Commercial No. 1
1. Children usually do not like spinach no matter what brand it is.
2. MEIJER shoppers like the store's higher prices and lower quality.
3. MEIJER shoppers appreciate the store's high quality and low prices.

TV Commercial No. 2
1. When MEIJER customers are shopping, they don't care about their children.
2. Shopping at a MEIJER supermarket is always a joy because of the low prices and high quality.
3. No matter how unattractive their daughters' boyfriends may be, parents always enjoy meeting them.

9. Utilizing Useful Words and Phrases: *Rearrange the words/phrases in parentheses below to make complete English sentences. Then translate the sentences into Japanese.*

1. Please (take / has just / Mary / the / a bite / baked / of / bread).

2. (don't / why / eat / the / restaurant / you / at / new / Italian)?

3. Can I (my / Sunday / boyfriend / bring / dinner / for / by / on)?

4. I've (a lot / for / shopping / do / my mother / to / more / got) this afternoon.

10. Optional Activity: *Read your completed transcripts (from Task 7 above) aloud as you watch the commercials with the sound off. Match the words with the action.*

11. Topics for Discussion: *Discuss the following topics in class, or write a short paragraph expressing your ideas on each topic.*

1. Spinach is one of the vegetables that children typically do not like. Can you think of any other vegetables children don't care for? Why do you think they dislike them?

2. "Sweetie" is an expression used to address a person's wife/husband, daughter/son, girlfriend/boyfriend, or other loved one. Can you think of any other similar expressions?

3. Would you invite your daughter's boyfriend or your son's girlfriend to dinner even if he or she was unfriendly or impolite?

Unit 2

This Calls for a Bud Light

©2004 Bud Light (Silver Lion)

I. Preliminary Reading: *This section provides preliminary background information for the TV commercial you are going to watch and listen to. Read the passage carefully and do the tasks that follow.*

There was once an American who was known as "The Wizard of Menlo Park." He was not a real wizard, of course, but the citizens of Menlo Park, New Jersey, called him that anyway because they were amazed that he had invented so many incredible devices —devices that would go on to greatly affect life all over the world in the 19th and 20th centuries. One of the inventions that proved to be a highlight of his life was the phonograph, or the prototype of sound recorders, without which we would not be able to enjoy listening to music on our small, portable music players today. Another of his important inventions was the long-lasting light bulb, which has enabled us to work, study, and play at night. This "wizard" is said to have held more than 1,000 patents, making him one of the most prolific inventors in history. His name is, as you have probably guessed, Thomas Alva Edison.

Another fact which amazes us about this great inventor is that he only went to school for three months altogether because his teacher considered him to be lacking in the ability to learn. His mother educated him instead, and, when he was only twelve, he started working as a newspaper sales boy. But he studied hard on his own and made a career as a telegraph operator. As his inventions became more popular in the U.S., the name Edison became a household word. Thomas was not, however, what we would call a genius. It is said that he tested over 3,000 filaments before he came up with a practical, long-lasting light bulb. According to his most famous quotation, "Genius is 99 percent perspiration and 1 percent inspiration." Edison himself is a case in point.

2. Vocabulary Build-up: *Find the highlighted words in the reading that match the following descriptions and write them in the parentheses, as in the example.*

Example: **A person who has great natural ability**   (*genius*   )
1. A person with magical skills   (   )
2. To make something never made before   (   )
3. An original model or first standard   (   )
4. Highly productive and creative   (   )
5. Something said by a famous person   (   )

3. Reading Comprehension: *Choose the sentence below which most closely matches the content of the reading passage.*

1. Thomas A. Edison was a professor from Menlo Park, New Jersey, who invented many fantastic devices such as the phonograph and the long-lasting light bulb.
2. Life today would be very different if Edison had not invented the phonograph, the light bulb, and all his other marvelous inventions.
3. Edison was a good student and, after graduating from high school, became a telegraph operator. Later on, he invented many wonderful devices.
4. Edison was not what we would call a true genius, because he often made mistakes and failed miserably many times.

Tasks for the TV Commercial

4. Vocabulary Preview: *Here are some key words/phrases you need to know to understand the TV commercial for this lesson. Match each with a word/phrase of similar meaning in the box below.*

1. institute   (   )   2. innovative   (   )   3. fascinating   (   )
4. fake   (   )   5. burn the midnight oil   (   )

> a. new   b. association; school   c. work late at night
> d. attractive   e. imitation

5. Soundtrack Listening (1): *Listen to the soundtrack of the commercial without looking at the screen. Then number the words/phrases/sentences below in the order in which you hear them. You can replay the soundtrack as many times as you like. Two have been done for you as examples.*

a. At the Bud Light Institute (1)
b. Where's Johnson? ( )
c. What new products ( )
d. Burning the midnight oil ( )
e. Maybe having a Bud Light ( )
f. A steaming cup of coffee on his desk ( )
g. Science. Working, so (7)

6. Soundtrack Listening (2): *Listen to the soundtrack again and put the words/phrases in parentheses below into the correct order to make sentences from the commercial.*

1. Let's take (into / a / future / look / the / fascinating).

   _____

2. What new (on / products / are / working / scientists / your)?

   _____

3. To the non-scientific eye this (like / coffee / cup / an / ordinary / may / look / of).

   _____

4. It is in fact a clever fake that (be / set / at / steaming / can / to start) 8 a.m.

   _____

7. Scene Description: *Watch the commercial and answer the following questions.*

1. What is Dr. Lindenburgs wearing?

   _____

2. What does Johnson's boss look like?

   _____

3. What is Johnson actually doing at 8:00 in the morning?

   _____

4. What is Johnson actually doing at 2:30 in the afternoon?

   _____

5. What is Johnson actually doing at 9:00 in the evening?

   _____

8. **Transcript Completion:** *As you watch and listen to the commercial again, fill in the blanks in the transcript below.*

Here at the Bud Light Institute _____ to finding _____ _____ of getting guys together with their friends and _____ a Bud Light.

Let's _____ into the future.

—Dr. Lindenburgs. What _____ are your scientists _____ _____?

—Well, Keith. To the non- _____ this may _____ _____. It is _____ that _____ _____ at 8 a.m.

—Wow.

—_____ Johnson's _____.

—Where's Johnson?

—I don't know, but there's _____.

—Johnson, _____ again.

—Science. Working, so _____.

This _____ a Bud Light.

9. **Utilizing Useful Words and Phrases:** *Rearrange the words/phrases in parentheses below to make complete English sentences. Then translate the sentences into Japanese.*

1. We are (poor / helping / committed / to / children / these).

2. The police (the suspect / a close look / of / the movements / into / took).

3. (sister / used to / the midnight / burn / oil / my) when she was studying to enter college.

4. (for / a / this / celebration / calls).

14

10. Optional Activity: *Read your completed transcript (from Task 8 above) aloud as you watch the commercial with the sound off. Match the words with the action.*

11. Topics for Discussion: *Discuss the following topics in class, or write a short paragraph expressing your ideas on each topic.*

1. Can you think of any gimmicks like the fake coffee cup that would help you avoid work?

2. In most Western corporations, employees have their own office, or at least a small, private cubicle, like the one seen in this TV commercial. Do you think this is the right policy?

3. Go to the Internet or library and find out about the legal drinking age in various countries and compare them with that of Japan.

Unit 3

Anti-Discrimination Campaign

I. Preliminary Reading: *This section provides preliminary background information for the TV commercial you are going to watch and listen to. Read the passage carefully and do the tasks that follow.*

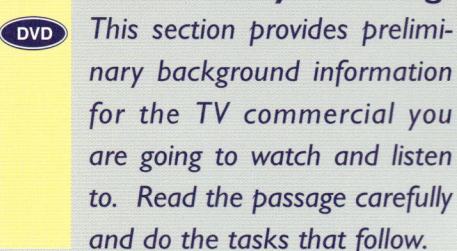

©2004 Gay Rights Campaign (Bronze Lion)

There was once an isolated ape kingdom located somewhere on this planet. One thing which characterized the kingdom was that all the apes there were three-eyed. One day an ape from another kingdom lost his way and entered the three-eyed kingdom. All the apes there began to bully the newcomer because he only had two eyes.
5 Since the three-eyed apes had never been outside of their kingdom, they believed that all apes were three-eyed and thought of the ape with two eyes as totally alien to them. He was never accepted as a member of three-eyed ape society, even though he insisted that he was an ordinary ape and that all his family and friends back in his homeland were two-eyed just like him.

10 Discrimination prevails everywhere in the world. Bullying at school is a major problem that worries teachers and parents in many countries today. Problems like this originate from human nature. People have two different feelings: one is that we want to be different from others or outstanding; the other is that we want to feel secure as a member of a certain group or community. Discrimination and bullying are actions
15 taken to protect the group or community we belong to, but in reality they are a primitive, inhumane, and shameful form of conduct in modern society. We live in an advanced, cultivated, and educated society where we should accept differences of all kinds: color of skin, place of birth, language, religion, political preference, physical characteristics, and sexual orientation. We should not be like the apes from the three-eyed
20 kingdom.

2. Vocabulary Build-up: *Find the highlighted words in the reading that match the following descriptions and write them in the parentheses, as in the example.*

Example: A large monkey with no tail (ape   )
1. Strange or foreign (   )
2. A country ruled by a king or queen (   )
3. To try to control others by threats or violence (   )
4. Prejudice or favoritism (   )
5. To begin or start (   )

3. Reading Comprehension: *Choose the sentence below which most closely matches the content of the reading passage.*

1. Once upon a time, three-eyed apes were seldom seen on this planet because two-eyed apes were more prevalent.
2. The two-eyed ape was bullied by the three-eyed apes because he had lost his way.
3. Discrimination and bullying are examples of cultivated and educated conduct that originate in human nature.
4. People today must not be like the three-eyed apes, but should learn to accept differences of all kinds.

Tasks for the TV Commercial

4. Vocabulary Preview: *Here are some key words you need to know to understand the TV commercial for this lesson. Match each with a word/phrase of similar meaning in the box below.*

1. automotive (   )   2. compose (   )   3. opportunity (   )
4. bother (   )   5. solely (   )

> a. chance   b. of cars   c. trouble   d. simply   e. write

5. Soundtrack Listening: *Listen to the soundtrack of the commercial without looking at the screen. Then number the words/phrases below in the order in which you hear them. You can replay the soundtrack as many times as you like. Two have been done for you as examples.*

a. My name   (1)   f. Forty-seven   (   )
b. I am gay   (   )   g. In the state I live in   (   )
c. Phil and Bob   (   )   h. The automotive industry   (   )
d. Why bother?   (   )   i. Composing an e-mail   (   )
e. More open and honest   (   )   j. A little scary   (10)

Unit 3

6. Story Line Completion: *The sentences below describe the scenes in the commercial for this lesson. Watch the video and then complete the commercial's story line by numbering the sentences in the order in which the scenes appear, as in the examples.*

1. A man is walking among automobile bodies in the factory. (1)
2. The man is reading his message on the memo pad. ( )
3. The man is walking outside the office. ( )
4. The man is writing something on a memo pad with a pen. ( )
5. The man is talking to the camera again. ( )
6. The man is typing his message on the keyboard of the computer. ( )
7. The man is talking to the camera looking at the memo pad. ( )
8. The man is typing his message on the computer again. (8)

7. Scene Description: *Watch the commercial again and answer the following questions.*

1. What does Steve look like?

   _____

2. Where is he composing his e-mail?

   _____

3. What is he doing in the last scene of the commercial?

   _____

8. Transcript Completion: *As you watch and listen to the commercial again, fill in the blanks in the transcript below.*

My name is Steve. _____. I work in the _____ of the _____. And right now _____ an e-mail _____ and my boss's boss. It says, Phil and Bob, I wanted to _____ that I am gay. I'm _____ and honest about _____ here at work. People would ask "Why bother?" "Why bother?" is because _____. At the same time, _____ in the state I live in solely _____. So, that's ah . . . that's it. It's kinda . . . a little scary but I'm gonna do it.

9. Finding the Commercial's Message: *Choose the sentence which best expresses the main message of the TV commercial.*

1. Steve is sending an e-mail to his boss and his boss's boss because they are gay.
2. There is no discrimination against workers based on their sexual orientation in any U.S. state.
3. We should all take action against discrimination of all kinds.
4. Steve is ashamed of being gay so he wants to quit his job.

10. Utilizing Useful Words and Phrases: *Rearrange the words/phrases in parentheses below to make complete English sentences. Then translate the sentences into Japanese.*

1. (opportunity / you / to take / know / to let / I'd / like / this) that I am going to get married next month.

2. Our government is taking (this / warming / to prevent / action / in / global / order).

3. The company (background / of / on / my educational / the basis / hired me).

4. He was (solely / he is / fired / because / from / his job) a Muslim.

11. Optional Activity: *Read your completed transcript (from Task 8 above) aloud as you watch the commercial with the sound off. Match the words with the action.*

12. Topics for Discussion: *Discuss the following topics in class, or write a short paragraph expressing your ideas on each topic.*

1. Is Steve making a mistake by doing something that could cost him his job?

2. Is Japan a society which is hospitable to the mentally and physically disabled?

3. Visit <TurnOut.org>. How does what you learn there make you feel?

Unit 4

McDonald's—King of Fast-Food Restaurants

1. Preliminary Reading: *This section provides preliminary background information for the TV commercials you are going to watch and listen to. Read the passage carefully and do the tasks that follow.*

©2002 McDonald's (Bronze Lion)

　　Americans eat so many hamburgers—for lunch or dinner, at picnics and family reunions , at birthday parties and sporting events and all kinds of other occasions—that the hamburger is often called America's national food. When and how did the hamburger get its name? In the 19th century, immigrants coming to the U.S. from
5　Hamburg, Germany, brought the food with them, and it soon caught on.

　　Hamburgers are so popular that at least one hamburger restaurant can be found on almost every street corner in most large U.S. cities. Some major U.S. hamburger restaurant chains have expanded their business to many countries, and now the hamburger is not only the favorite food of Americans, but it is also very popular with
10　Russians, Chinese, Japanese, Mexicans, Egyptians, Australians, and many others.

　　The biggest hamburger restaurant chain is, as you can easily guess, McDonald's, which was founded in 1940 in San Bernardino, California. Today, McDonald's has as many as 31,000 locations worldwide. Burger King, the second biggest chain, was founded in 1954 in Miami, Florida, and has expanded to over 11,000 franchise stores.
15　Wendy's, founded in 1969 in Columbus, Ohio, ranks third, with approximately 6,700 restaurants around the world.

　　The hamburger, often served together with French fries, is tasty and substantial enough to satisfy the appetites of hungry children. One of McDonald's competitors , KFC, or Kentucky Fried Chicken, also offers an attractive menu that appeals to chil-
20　dren. These fast-food restaurants are, however, sometimes criticized by health-conscious mothers and fathers because they offer high-calorie menus which could lead to their children becoming obese .

　　Even though obesity has become a big social issue in many advanced countries, fast foods are more in demand than ever these days because of the need for appetizing
25　meals served in a minimum amount of time.

2. **Vocabulary Build-up:** *Find the highlighted words in the reading that match the following descriptions and write them in the parentheses, as in the example.*

   Example: About (*approximately*)
   1. A desire to drink or eat ( )
   2. A gathering or meeting of relatives or former classmates ( )
   3. Very fat ( )
   4. People who move to another country ( )
   5. The least amount ( )

3. **Reading Comprehension:** *Choose the sentence below which most closely matches the content of the reading passage.*
   1. The most typical American food is called a "hamburger" because so many Germans visited the United States in the 19th century.
   2. Today, the hamburger is not the only American national food; there are many other dishes that are just as popular.
   3. Burger King is the third-biggest hamburger restaurant chain in Miami, Florida, and has over 11,000 stores there.
   4. Despite their popularity and convenience, fast-food restaurants are often criticized for serving high-calorie foods which can make children fat.

Tasks for TV Commercials No. 1 and No. 2

4. **Vocabulary Preview:** *Here are some key words you need to know to understand the TV commercials for this lesson. Match each with a word of similar meaning in the box below.*

   1. promotion ( ) 2. research ( ) 3. evaluation ( )
   4. identical ( ) 5. campaign ( )

   > a. same   b. movement   c. study   d. advertising   e. rating

5. **Soundtrack Listening:** *Listen to the soundtracks of TV Commercials No. 1 and No. 2 without looking at the screen. Then number the words/phrases/sentences below in the order in which you hear them. You can replay the soundtracks as many times as you like. Two have been done for you as examples.*

   TV Commercial No.1
   a. Brushed your teeth (1)
   b. How about when you come back? ( )
   c. Mom's taking me ( )
   d. By two, OK? ( )
   e. Come here ( )
   f. Dad's taking me ( )
   g. How about you and me ( )

   TV Commercial No.2
   a. Here at McDonald's (1)
   b. Last Christmas ( )
   c. Quite good ( )
   d. A Coca-Cola glass ( )
   e. Not this time ( )
   f. A successful promotion ( )
   g. For us ( )

6. Story Line Completion: *The sentences below describe the scenes in the commercials for this lesson. Watch the video and then complete the commercials' story lines by numbering the sentences in the order in which the scenes appear, as in the examples.*

TV Commercial No. 1

1. The mother is helping her son put on his coat. (1)
2. The father and his son have a short chat in the car. (　)
3. The mother is brushing her son's hair. (　)
4. The father and his son head for McDonald's. (　)
5. The father is standing beside his car waiting for his son. (　)
6. The boy runs and gets into his father's car. (　)

TV Commercial No. 2

1. A shimmering campaign slogan (1)
2. A shimmering McDonald's logo (　)
3. The upper half of an empty Coca-Cola glass (　)
4. A hamburger, French fries, and drink (　)
5. A whole Coca-Cola glass (　)

7. Transcript Completion: *As you watch and listen to the commercials again, fill in the blanks in the transcripts below.*

TV Commercial No. 1

Mother:	Have you _____ yet, Dennis?
Dennis:	Yeeeees.
Mother:	_____. You haven't had your _____.
Dennis:	Dad's _____.
Mother:	Oh, _____? Well, how about _____, you and me _____?
Dennis:	Yeah!
Father:	That's it.
Mother:	I need him _____, OK?
Father:	_____ at two o'clock?
Dennis:	Emm..., _____ to the zoo.
Father:	Well, _____ you and me _____?
Dennis:	Yeah!

TV Commercial No. 2

Here	, every time	we
always do, you know,	, testing,	. Not
. The idea		with every Maxi menu
	an identical campaign	did
	. And we thought	. So if it worked
,	shouldn't it work	?

8. Finding the Commercial's Message: *Choose the sentence that best expresses the main message of each commercial.*

TV Commercial No. 1

1. Both the boy's mother and father want to take their son to McDonald's because they like the menu.
2. Even though the boy's mother and father are separated, they always want to take their son to McDonald's because they love him so much.
3. Both parents want to take their son to McDonald's because they want to do what pleases their son most—and what makes him love them more.

TV Commercial No. 2

1. At McDonald's, each time you order a Maxi menu, you get a free Coca-Cola glass, a promotion that was first successfully used by a competitor.
2. Last Christmas, Coca-Cola ran an identical campaign as McDonald's did and it was very successful.
3. It took a lot of hard work and research for McDonald's to come up with its Coca-Cola glass give-away campaign.

9. Utilizing Useful Words and Phrases: *Rearrange the words/phrases in parentheses below to make complete English sentences. Then translate the sentences into Japanese.*

1. (father's / about / how / your / visiting / office) tomorrow morning?

   _____

   _____

2. (going / over / what's / there/ on) on the street corner?

   _____

   _____

3. (of / we / lot / a / research / do) when we open a new branch.

4. The idea (last year's / promotion / actually / from / campaign / came).

5. If the campaign worked for them, (our / why / for /company / shouldn't / work / it)?

10. **Optional Activity:** *Read your completed transcripts (from Task 7 above) aloud as you watch the commercials with the sound off. Match the words with the action.*

11. **Topics for Discussion:** *Discuss the following questions in class, or write a short paragraph expressing your ideas on each topic.*

1. Why does the boy in TV Commercial No.1 lie to his father?

2. What kind of promotion items have you received from fast-food restaurants? Do such promotions really help attract customers?

3. Is fast food really the main cause of obesity?

4. How would you describe the house where the mother and son live?

Relax, it's FedEx.

Unit 5

©2004 FedEx (Gold Lion)

I. Preliminary Reading:
This section provides preliminary background information for the TV commercials you are going to watch and listen to. Read the passage carefully and do the tasks that follow.

    The first modern postal service was started in Britain in 1840. Since then, most countries have introduced and developed their own postal service systems, and now issue their own stamps. The Universal Postal Union was established in 1847 in Bern, Switzerland, to ensure that mail is delivered to any of the UPU member countries if it is properly stamped and posted. The UPU is now an organization of the United Nations.

    Apart from the postal service, many other convenient communication systems and devices have been developed, such as the telegraph, the facsimile machine, the telephone, and now the Internet. These have greatly altered the traditional mail delivery system. The role of the postal letter has also changed. Once a major means of communication, the letter now plays a more formal and sophisticated role. Regular mail is now often called "snail mail" because it takes days to reach the receiver, while an e-mail arrives in less than a second.

    Of course, these new communication means and devices can only deliver text; they are not capable of delivering articles or packages, which must still be handled by the mail service.

    Most postal systems were originally developed as public or governmental organizations. Today, however, private companies have been taking over their monopolistic place because national delivery systems have become increasingly inefficient. These new privately-run systems operate in accordance with the development of the society they serve and have become quite successful in many countries. FedEx, founded as Federal Express in 1971 by Fred Smith, is one such system.

2. **Vocabulary Build-up:** Find the highlighted words in the reading that match the following descriptions and write them in the parentheses, as in the example.

   Example: A tool or machine made for a particular purpose (*device*)
   1. To begin or set up something ( )
   2. An object or box wrapped in paper ( )
   3. To take letters or parcels to the places they are addressed to ( )
   4. Job to do or part to play ( )
   5. In a correct way ( )

3. **Reading Comprehension:** Choose the sentence below which most closely matches the content of the reading passage.

   1. If your mail is properly stamped and posted, it will be delivered to the Universal Postal Union in Bern, Switzerland.
   2. The postal service system's role has changed from a more formal and sophisticated means of communication to an increasingly important and popular one.
   3. New communication devices are now capable of delivering articles or packages which are at present still handled by the postal service.
   4. As governmental or public delivery systems became less efficient in many countries, private businesses began taking their place.

Tasks for TV Commercials No. 1 and No. 2

4. **Vocabulary Preview:** Here are some key words/phrases you need to know to understand the TV commercials for this lesson. Match each with a word/phrase of similar meaning in the box below.

   1. a bit of ( ) 2. jam ( ) 3. shipping ( ) 4. remind ( ) 5. reliable ( )

   > a. dependable   b. a little   c. trouble   d. sending   e. tell again

5. **Soundtrack Listening:** Listen to the soundtracks of TV commercials No. 1 and No. 2 without looking at the screen. Then number the words/phrases/sentences below in the order in which you hear them. You can replay the soundtracks as many times as you like. Two have been done for you as examples.

   TV Commercial No. 1
   a. This morning (1)
   b. FedEx Express ( )
   c. Relax ( )
   d. Around here ( )
   e. My dad ( )
   f. Few days late ( )

   TV Commercial No. 2
   a. Use your help (1)
   b. Even an MBA ( )
   c. Get out today ( )
   d. How to do it ( )
   e. Very easy ( )
   f. Don't understand ( )
   g. Don't do shipping ( )
   h. A bit of a jam ( )

6. Story Line Completion: *The sentences below describe the scenes in TV Commercial No. 2. Watch the video and then complete the commercial's story line by numbering the sentences in the order in which the scenes appear.*

TV Commercial No. 2
1. They go into the shipping department. ( )
2. Both the woman and the man leave his office. ( )
3. The woman shows the man how to use the computer. ( )
4. The man sits down at the computer desk. ( )
5. A woman comes into a young employee's office and asks a favor. ( )

7. Scene Description: *Watch the commercials again and answer the following questions.*

TV Commercial No. 1
1. What is the young man doing when his boss comes into the office?

2. What is the boss's reaction when the young man says, "You're my dad"?

TV Commercial No. 2
1. What does the young man do when he leaves his office?

2. What does the young man do as he is walking along the corridor?

8. Transcript Completion: *Listen to the soundtracks again and put the words/phrases in parentheses below into the correct order to make sentences from the commercials.*

TV Commercial No. 1
1. Did (this / Detroit / get / those / to / morning / shipments)?

2. Did you (you / like / Express / use / FedEx / asked / I)?

3. Remind me (you / here / again / I / keep / why / around)?

TV Commercial No. 2

1. I know it's your first day, but (we/ use / could / really / your / help).

2. Thanks, (in / of / a / just / we're / bit / a / jam).

3. In that case (to / show / to / you / how / I'll / have / do / it).

9. Utilizing Useful Words and Phrases: *Rearrange the words/phrases in parentheses below to make complete English sentences. Then translate the sentences into Japanese.*

1. Did you (I asked / like / new / use / the / you / system)?

2. Please (why / a meeting / we / remind us / have) every Monday morning.

3. We have just moved into our new office, (a / so / are / we / jam / in / terrible).

4. In that case (show / you / will / the problem / how / the boss / to solve).

10. Optional Activity: *Read your completed partial transcript (from Task 8 above) aloud as you watch the commercials with the sound off. Match the words with the action.*

11. Topics for Discussion: *Discuss the following topics in class, or write a short paragraph expressing your ideas on each topic.*

1. What do you think the punch line, "Even an MBA can do it" means?

2. Are personal connections helpful everywhere when looking for a job?

BMW—A Car beyond Reason

Unit 6

1. Preliminary Reading: *This section provides preliminary background information for the TV commercial you are going to watch and listen to. Read the passage carefully and do the tasks that follow.*

©2000 BMW Iberica (Bronze Lion)

  The word "ordinary" is difficult to define. To some people, being classed as an ordinary person is quite acceptable, but to others being regarded as ordinary is thought to be boring or rude or unsatisfactory. But the word covers a fairly good percentage of all people, although the ratio of ordinary/extraordinary varies from place to place and from society to society.

  What is an ordinary person's dream in life? Many dream of owning their own "home." The home might stand on a sunny hillside and have a beautiful view. The home includes a kind, hard-working husband and a wife who is always on hand taking care of or playing with the healthy, beautiful children. Keeping a dog makes the dream seem more realistic, and having a luxury car standing in the carport completes the picture.

  This picture, however, may be a little traditional or conservative these days because the meaning of the word "ordinary" has been changing in accordance with changes in society. The image of the "home" has altered as the number of single-parent families has increased. In many developed countries, birthrates are decreasing, which means that each family has fewer children.

  The word "DINKS" was once a fashionable word used to describe a couple with "double income, no kids." Both partners worked and they intentionally did not have children so that they could live a free and luxurious life. This word, however, is not used so often these days as it once was. This lifestyle has become just one of many other modern family types, such as the single-parent family, or divorced and remarried parents living with stepsons or stepdaughters, or same-sex couples living with adopted children. However, no matter how complicated society may become, the basic function of the home stays the same: maintaining the smallest unit of the community as part of the nation at large.

2. Vocabulary Build-up: *Find the* highlighted *words in the reading that match the following descriptions and write them in the parentheses, as in the example.*

    Example: To a certain extent   (fairly   )
    1. To finish making or doing something   (   )
    2. Opposed to social change   (   )
    3. Difficult to understand   (   )
    4. To take someone else's child into your family   (   )
    5. To describe exactly   (   )

3. Reading Comprehension: *Choose the sentence below which most closely matches the content of the reading passage.*

1. While some people accept being regarded as ordinary, many others are not very satisfied or pleased with being seen as an ordinary person.
2. Having a luxury car and keeping a dog does nothing to make the ordinary person's dream in life seem more realistic.
3. The image of the "home" has been changing rapidly along with the increase in the number of single-parent and other non-traditional families.
4. The word "DINKS" is still often used these days because the basic function of the home always stays the same.

Tasks for the TV Commercial

4. Vocabulary Preview: *Here are some key words you need to know to understand the TV commercial for this lesson. Match each with a word of similar meaning in the box below.*

    1. shelter   ( )   2. ensure   ( )   3. entire   ( )   4. tenderness ( )
    5. intelligence ( )   6. commotion ( )   7. companion ( )

> a. protect   b. friend   c. whole   d. knowledge
>   e. softness   f. disorder   g. guarantee

5. Soundtrack Listening: *Listen to the soundtrack of the commercial without looking at the screen. Then number the words/phrases/sentences below in the order in which you hear them. You can replay the soundtrack as many times as you like.*

    a. My car   ( )
    b. Facing south-south east   ( )
    c. Perfect balance   ( )
    d. Understanding spirit   ( )
    e. Stand up to the summer heat   ( )
    f. An excellent companion   ( )

6. Story Line Completion: *The sentences below describe the scenes in the commercial. Watch the video and then complete the commercial's story line by numbering the sentences in the order in which the scenes appear.*

1. The man is standing in front of his BMW in the backyard. ( )
2. The man is patting his dog. ( )
3. A woman is putting nail polish on her toes. ( )
4. The man and woman are standing side by side. ( )
5. The man is with his son and daughter. ( )
6. The man takes a few steps in his front yard. ( )
7. A tall, slim man is standing in front of his house. ( )

7. Scene Description: *Watch the commercial again and answer the following questions.*

1. What is the owner's wife doing when he introduces her?

   _____

2. Describe the owner's children.

   _____

8. Transcript Completion: *As you watch and listen to the commercial again, fill in the blanks in the partial transcript below.*

1. My house—I chose it because it's sheltered _____ and _____ _____, facing south-south east, ensures _____.
2. My wife—_____ for _____, tenderness, intelligence, and _____.
3. My children—I had two because it's _____ the loneliness _____ and the excessive commotion _____.
4. My dog—_____ because the breed make _____—and is an excellent _____.
5. My lawn—I chose this grass because _____ and can _____ _____ and the frosts _____.

Unit 6   31

9. **Utilizing Useful Words and Phrases:** *Rearrange the words/phrases in parentheses below to make complete English sentences. Then translate the sentences into Japanese.*

   1. Our home faces (sheltered / south / but is / summer / from / heat / the).

   2. I employed him (of honesty / for / language ability / combination / and / his).

   3. We chose Pierre as (class leader / he / strong / because /our / showed / leadership) abilities.

   4. The police chose (good / German Shepherds / they / because / make / police dogs).

10. **Optional Activity:** *Read your completed partial transcript (from Task 8 above) aloud as you watch the commercials with the sound off. Match the words with the action.*

11. **Topics for Discussion:** *Discuss the following topics in class, or write a short paragraph expressing your ideas on each topic.*

    1. Why doesn't the owner of the house explain why he has a BMW?

    2. What is your definition of the ideal family?

    3. Where would you like to have your dream house built?

Unit 7

Banking for the Filthy Rich

©2000 CyberCash -Stared at (Gold Lion)

I. Preliminary Reading: *This section provides preliminary background information for the TV commercials you are going to watch and listen to. Read the passage carefully and do the tasks that follow.*

Pierre was born in New Caledonia, and lives in a shack on the beach. His income is about nine hundred US dollars a year, but he has a lot of leisure time and enjoys talking with his family and friends all day in the beautiful tropical sunshine—with not a worry in the world.

James, a stock trader working on Wall Street, commutes to the office in his Mercedes SL, wears a 5,000-dollar Italian suit, works under unbelievably high pressure, and can make or lose billions of dollars in a flash. He has no time to spare in his life, not one second.

Nabil was born as the first son of a Saudi Arabian family and is now living in a huge white mansion surrounded by a vast yard covered with green grass and lined with high palm trees. Nabil went to school in Britain and graduated from Oxford, but he can't choose the job he wants because he must join his family business.

Pierre envies James, as James does Nabil. Nabil often envies Pierre. As the old maxim says, the grass is always greener on the other side of the fence. We all have scales for measuring other people's happiness, but usually not for our own. Feeling happy is often a matter of comparison.

Most problems in the world can be said to occur as a result of the economic divide between the haves and the have-nots. This divide or gap has been growing wider and wider, which means that the world is becoming more and more unstable and insecure.

Now is the time for us to stop looking at things from an economic viewpoint only. Otherwise, with the rapidly increasing world population, it will be impossible for everyone to own a comfortable, air-conditioned house, drive a big, expensive car, and eat nourishing food. All of these are energy-consuming and carbon dioxide-producing elements. The limit of Planet Earth to feed and house all its people is just around the corner. Where do you stand on this matter? Are you an economist or an ecologist?

2. Vocabulary Build-up: Find the highlighted words in the reading that match the following descriptions and write them in the parentheses, as in the example.

Example: To happen (*occure*)
1. Very large ( )
2. A big, private house ( )
3. To be jealous of ( )
4. To go back and forth to school or work ( )
5. Healthy, wholesome, or nutritious ( )

3. Reading Comprehension: Choose the sentence below which most closely matches the content of the reading passage.

1. James works under unbelievably high pressure and has no time to talk with family and friends.
2. Nabil went to school in Britain and graduated from Oxford, so he has not been able to join his family business.
3. The economic divide between the rich and the poor has been growing wider, which is making the world increasingly unstable.
4. Air conditioners and big cars are energy-producing and carbon dioxide-consuming elements.

Tasks for TV Commercials No. 1 and No. 2

4. Vocabulary Preview: Here are some key words you need to know to understand the TV commercials for this lesson. Match each with a word of similar meaning in the box below.

1. neighborhood ( )   2. avoid ( )   3. struggle ( )
4. consider ( )   5. stare ( )   6. filthy ( )

| a. think | b. escape | c. extremely | d. community | e. fight | f. look |

5. Soundtrack Listening: Listen to the soundtrack of TV Commercials No. 1 and No. 2 without looking at the screen. Then number the words/phrases/sentences below in the order in which you hear them. You can replay the soundtrack as many times as you like. Two have been done for you as examples.

TV Commercial No. 1
a. Stared at (1)
b. Eat in restaurants ( )
c. One of them ( )
d. Laughed at ( )
e. A lonely existence ( )
f. Little choice ( )
g. Filthy rich ( )

TV Commercial No. 2
a. Neighborhood (1)
b. Go out of your way ( )
c. Happen to you ( )
d. What they have ( )
e. Some kind of life ( )
f. Different ( )
g. Just like you ( )

6. Story Line Completion: *The sentences below describe the scenes in the commercials for this lesson. Watch the video and then complete the commercials' story lines by numbering the sentences in the order in which the scenes appear, as in the examples.*

TV Commercial No. 1
1. An elderly couple are eating in a fancy restaurant. (   )
2. An elderly woman wearing a red cloak is taking a walk with two white dogs. (   )
3. The gate is opening to let a red sports car into a huge walled compound. (3)
4. A man is mounted on a horse with several hunting dogs beside him. (   )
5. A man and woman are riding on a motorbike beside a Rolls Royce. (   )

TV Commercial No. 2
1. A butler is picking up the newspaper from the driveway in front of a stately mansion. (   )
2. A woman in a bathing suit at poolside is taking a glass from a tray. (   )
3. A doorman is carrying a woman's boxes to her car. (   )
4. Children are getting out of expensive cars and entering a school building. (   )
5. An elderly man is closing the door. (   )
6. A middle-aged man with a beard starts talking to the camera. (1)
7. Some people are playing croquet on the lawn. (   )

7. Scene Description: *Watch Commercial No. 1 again and answer the following questions.*

TV Commercial No. 1
1. What is the elderly woman with the white dogs holding in her right hand?

2. What is the waiter in the restaurant doing?

3. Describe the man mounted on the horse.

4. Who is looking through the gate at the outside world?

8. **Transcript Completion:** *As you watch and listen to the commercials again, fill in the blanks in the transcripts below.*

   TV Commercial No. 1

They are _____. They are _____. Many _____ but to live in walled compounds, to _____ just _____. It can be _____. Who are these people? The filthy rich. _____, by _____?

   TV Commercial No. 2

It's _____ you _____ in. _____, you might _____ to avoid it. But _____ live here—flesh and blood humans, _____. They _____ what they have, struggling to _____ for themselves. And yet _____ different. You might even _____ them. It's time to give the rich _____. After all, _____ to you.

9. **Utilizing Useful Words and Phrases:** *Rearrange the words/phrases in parentheses below to make complete English sentences. Then translate the sentences into Japanese.*

   1. The people had (but / little / to / choice / the dictator / obey).

   2. (was / stared at / the man / at / because / and laughed) he was wearing a pink suit.

   3. (went / the children / out of / to avoid / their way) the barking dog.

   4. It's (to / give / time / some / assistance / economic / the poor).

10. Optional Activity: *Read your completed transcripts aloud as you watch the commercials with the sound off. Match the words with the action.*

11. Topics for Discussion: *Discuss the following topics in class, or write a short paragraph expressing your ideas on each topic.*

1. How much money would a person require to be considered "filthy rich"?

2. Name ten of the world's richest people.

3. What is your reaction when you see very rich people?

4. What would you do first if you were filthy rich?

Unit 8

Learning Languages

1. Preliminary Reading:

This section provides preliminary background information for the TV commercial you are going to watch and listen to. Read the passage carefully and do the tasks that follow.

©2005 Satellite TV Channel (Silver Lion)

Heinrich was born in Mecklenburg, Germany, in 1822. He was a very clever boy from his early childhood. His favorite books were *The Odyssey* and *The Iliad*, epic poems written by the great Greek poet, Homer. Heinrich was interested in Greek myths and the story of the Trojan War as described in *The Iliad*. He believed the epic to be true and hoped to one day find evidence proving that the Trojan War had really occurred.

When Heinrich was 14 years old, he finished school and started his career as a merchant dealing in foods and general goods. He was so talented and diligent that he eventually became a highly successful businessman and made a great fortune, on which he was able to live happily ever after. Upon retirement, he went on a two-year-long journey around the world, setting out from Germany, and stopping in Italy, Egypt, India, China, Japan, and Mexico. Later, when he was 42 years old, he decided to try to realize his dream by searching for the ruins of Troy.

The Aegean Civilization prospered from 3000 to 1200 BC in Greece and Turkey and in the islands that dotted the Aegean Sea. Most people believed the civilization to be only a legend until Heinrich started digging among the ruins and proved that it had actually existed. His first major discovery came in 1870 in Turkey, where he found many Trojan artifacts and treasures buried together with the kings of the ancient civilization.

Heinrich Schliemann, an amateur archaeologist, was able to fulfill his lifelong ambition because he worked very hard to build up his business and gain financial independence. His success was supported by his business partners from many places in Europe, the Middle East, and Russia, who said that it was Heinrich's outstanding language abilities that made it possible for him to maintain good human relationships with them. Indeed, Schliemann was a very keen language learner. While running his business he mastered several languages, including English, French, Dutch, Russian, Greek, Italian, and Latin. This should surely indicate to all of us that mastering languages can help open up many career paths for the future.

2. Vocabulary Build-up: *Find the highlighted words in the reading that match the following descriptions and write them in the parentheses, as in the example.*

Example: Proof (evidence)
1. To be successful and wealthy ( )
2. Non-professional ( )
3. Occupation or profession ( )
4. Very old ( )
5. Businessperson or storekeeper ( )

3. Reading Comprehension: *Choose the sentence below which most closely matches the content of the reading passage.*

1. Heinrich spent his early childhood in Greece and his lifelong dream was to find evidence that the Trojan War was an actual event.
2. Heinrich became a successful businessman and went on a two-year-long journey to find the ruins of Troy when he retired at 42 years old.
3. Heinrich's first discovery was in 1870 in Turkey, where he was buried together with the kings of ancient Troy.
4. Heinrich was able to maintain good human relationships with his business partners and fulfill his lifelong ambition because he was keen on languages.

Tasks for the TV Commercial

4. Vocabulary Preview: *Here are some key words you need to know to understand the TV commercial for this lesson. Match each with a word/phrase of similar meaning in the box below.*

1. concerns ( ) 2. obligatory ( ) 3. clarify ( )
4. pressure ( ) 5. environment ( )

| a. make clearer | b. burden | c. compulsory | d. surroundings | e. worries |

5. Soundtrack Listening: *Listen to the soundtrack of the commercial without looking at the screen. Then number the words/phrases/sentences below in the order in which you hear them. You can replay the sound track as many times as you like. Two have been done for you as examples.*

a. Your children's teacher (1)   f. Too young to learn another language ( )
b. French obligatory? ( )   g. Paragraph 1 ( )
c. Jenny's father ( )   h. German also? ( )
d. Let me clarify again. ( )   i. Your concerns ( )
e. Don't worry. ( )   j. In a normal environment (10)

Unit 8

6. Story Line Completion: *The sentences below describe the scenes in the commercial for this lesson. Watch the video and then complete the commercial's story line by numbering the sentences in the order in which the scenes appear.*

1. Jenny's father is happy with Mary's explanation about the foreign language program. ( )
2. The teacher starts to explain the foreign language program to the parents of her pupils. ( )
3. Mary introduces herself to her pupils' parents. ( )
4. Mary says that students must choose one of the three language options. ( )
5. Jenny's father asks a question about the French subject. ( )

7. Scene Description: *Watch the commercial again and answer the following questions.*

1. What can you see behind the teacher?

2. Describe the teacher.

3. What do you think Jenny's father's profession is?

8. Transcript Completion: *As you watch and listen to the commercial again, fill in the blanks in the transcript below.*

Teacher: My name is Mary and _____. Um, _____, paragraph 1, please, you will notice . . .

Man 1: _____. Hi everybody. I'm, ah, Jenny's father. _____ the French subject, really.

Teacher: What exactly are _____?

Man 1: Aren't they _____?

Man 2: Yeah, _____.

Teacher: _____. Recent studies have shown that _____, the easier it will _____.

Man 3: Is French obligatory?

Teacher: They can actually choose between _____.

Man 1: German also?

Teacher: Yes. However, _____, you must choose _____.

Man 1: Oh, _____, because _____ to grow up without pressure, in _____.

40

9. Utilizing Useful Words and Phrases: *Rearrange the words/phrases in parentheses below to make complete English sentences. Then translate the sentences into Japanese.*

1. Please (the / have / third / at / line / a look) on page 35 of the reference book.

2. At 13 years old, John (too / to / young / driver's / license / get / was / a).

3. (children / the / learning / start / younger / English), the faster they will master it.

4. (wanted / start / me / to / learning / my father / French) when I entered elementary school.

10. Optional Activity: *Read your completed transcript (from Task 8 above) aloud as you watch the commercial with the sound off. Match the words with the action.*

11. Topics for Discussion: *Discuss the following topics in class, or write a short paragraph expressing your ideas on each topic.*

1. How would you feel if your father acted like Jenny's father?

2. Why is the last phrase "in a normal environment" considered funny?

3. Is it a good idea to teach English to very young children?

Unit 8

Unit 9

Pepsi—Ask for More

1. Preliminary Reading: *This section provides preliminary background information for the TV commercials you are going to watch and listen to. Read the passage carefully and do the tasks that follow.*

©2003 Pepsi Cola—Elephant Tower (Bronze Lion)

Our ancestors invented a variety of beverages, including both alcoholic and non-alcoholic drinks. The three major alcoholic drinks are beer, wine, and whisky. Beer was first produced by the Babylonians about 4000 BC and is now the most popular. In most cases, beer is made from fermented barley, called malt, and given a slightly bitter flavor by adding hops. Wine is made from fermented grape juice. It was originally produced along the Rhine, Rhone, and Loire rivers in Europe. Whisky, also spelled whiskey, originated either in Scotland or in Ireland, and is distilled from fermented grain aged in oak barrels. Whisky often has an alcohol content of from 40 to 50 percent.

There are also a variety of non-alcoholic beverages such as fruit juice, coffee, tea, sodas, and colas. Juice, coffee, and tea are usually consumed at meal times, but sodas and colas are often reserved for leisure and recreational activities.

Cola is a unique drink in that it was originally invented for use as a medication. There are many local brands as well as major world brands like Coca-Cola and Pepsi. Both the Coca-Cola Co. and PepsiCo, Inc. are based in the U.S.A.; Coca-Cola was born in the state of Georgia in 1886, while Pepsi originated in North Carolina in 1898. Both companies have subsidiary networks that cover most of the world. Coke and Pepsi have long competed against each other utilizing mass media such as TV, radio, newspapers, and magazines to obtain a larger share of worldwide sales.

Ad campaigns for alcoholic drinks are often restricted by certain regulations because minors are banned from drinking alcohol. But soft drink ads are less limited, and the two major cola companies can usually be counted on to come up with highly creative commercials that win both customers and prizes.

2. **Vocabulary Build-up:** Find the highlighted words in the reading that match the following descriptions and write them in the parentheses, as in the example.

   Example: To change sugar into alcohol by adding yeast (ferment   )
   1. To extract the essential elements of (   )
   2. Playing a secondary or assisting role (   )
   3. Any drinkable liquid (   )
   4. A law or rule (   )
   5. Wheat, corn, rye, oats, rice, etc. (   )

3. **Reading Comprehension:** Choose the sentence below which most closely matches the content of the reading passage.

   1. Wine is made from fermented grape juice, and was first produced by the Babylonians about 4000 BC along the Rhine, Rhone, and Loire rivers.
   2. Whisky, originally produced either in Scotland or Ireland, is distilled from fermented barley, called malt, and flavored with oak.
   3. Both the Coca-Cola Co. and PepsiCo, Inc. have subsidiary networks all over the world and have long competed against each other to win customers through clever ad campaigns.
   4. Ad campaigns for beer and whisky are restricted by regulations, while Coca-Cola and Pepsi are even more restricted because minors are too young to drink them.

Tasks for TV Commercials No. 1 and No. 2

4. **Vocabulary Preview:** Here are some key words you need to know to understand the TV commercials for this lesson. Match each with a word of similar meaning in the box below.

   1. discover   (   )   2. train   (   )   3. referee   (   )
   4. determine   (   )   5. incredible   (   )   6. forever   (   )

   | a. decide   b. always   c. teach   d. unbelievable   e. judge   f. realize |

5. **Soundtrack Listening:** Listen to the soundtrack of TV Commercials No. 1 and No. 2 without looking at the screen. Then number the words/phrases/sentences below in the order in which you hear them. You can replay the soundtrack as many times as you like. Two have been done for you as examples.

   TV Commercial No. 1   *TV Commercial No. 2*
   a. I can remember   (1)   a. My father's dream   (1)
   b. All over India   (   )   b. In my blood   (   )
   c. With elephants   (   )   c. A referee   (   )
   d. The elephant tower   (   )   d. Laughed at me   (   )
   e. I am back   (   )   e. All the boys   (   )
   f. Not a good idea   (   )   f. Moment   (   )
   g. I discovered   (   )   g. Changed forever   (   )

6. Story Line Completion: *The sentences below describe the scenes in the commercials for this lesson. Watch the video and then complete the commercial's story lines by numbering the sentences in the order in which the scenes appear.*

TV Commercial No. 1
1. The young man is happy again because he has found another animal to train. (   )
2. The elephant tower falls when another small boy opens a can of Pepsi. (   )
3. Some elephant trainers are washing their elephants by the side of a lake or river. (   )
4. The boy is showing his elephant tower to the spectators at the circus. (   )
5. The boy is training some elephants to stand on one another's backs to make a tower. (   )
6. A small boy is teaching a small elephant tricks using a Pepsi can. (   )

TV Commercial No. 2
1. A jeep is driving along a rough country road. (   )
2. The boy kicked the falling can of Pepsi straight out the door of the shop. (   )
3. Another boy sticks his tongue out at the little boy on the street. (   )
4. The youngest boy is holding up a yellow card in the back of the car. (   )
5. A Pepsi can almost falls on the boy's mother's head while they are shopping. (   )
6. The boy is practicing to be a referee in front of a mirror. (   )
7. Ronaldinho, the little boy, now a famous football player, is playing soccer. (   )

7. Scene Description: *Watch the commercials again and answer the following questions.*

TV Commercial No. 1
1. Where is the boy as he watches the elephant trainers wash their elephants?

2. How many elephants does the tower in the circus consist of?

3. What is the next animal the boy is going to train?

TV Commercial No. 2
1. What is the boy wearing?

2. Why does the boy kick the Pepsi can?

3. What kind of kick did the boy use to kick the Pepsi can?

8. Transcript Completion: *As you watch and listen to the commercials again, fill in the blanks in the transcripts below.*

TV Commercial No. 1

1. As far as _____, I have always _____.
2. Then one day, I _____ over them, so I _____ to do something special.
3. The elephant tower. My elephant _____, and bigger.
4. I was famous _____.
5. But I _____ about _____.
6. Elephants were _____.
7. I think _____.

TV Commercial No. 2

1. It was _____, that _____ become footballers.
2. But I, I always _____. Yes, a referee.
3. My friends at school, _____; but I _____. To be a ref, was _____.
4. Till _____, that all changed. In _____ moment, _____.
5. If _____ Pepsi, I might have become _____.

9. Utilizing Useful Words and Phrases: *Rearrange the words/phrases in parentheses below to make complete English sentences. Then translate the sentences into Japanese.*

1. (Ronaldinho / as far / the best / know /as / I / is) soccer player in the world.

2. (wrong / about / I / was / my / new / boss), because she is really very kind.

3. (it / that / my brother / is / my mother's / dream) and I become doctors some day.

Unit 9

4. The knight said, "(against / in / my blood / evil / fighting / is)."

5. (it /not / if / for / had / been) your guidance, I might have become a criminal.

10. Optional Activity: *Read your completed transcripts (from Task 8 above) aloud as you watch the commercials with the sound off. Match the words with the action.*

11. Topics for Discussion: *Discuss the following topics in class, or write a short paragraph expressing your ideas on each topic.*

1. Apart from elephant trainers, name some other animal trainers or tamers you have seen in a circus or on TV.

2. When the boy in TV Commercial No. 2 meets the little boy in the street, the other boy sticks his tongue out at him. Is it also considered bad manners in your culture to stick out your tongue at someone?

3. What are some common hand gestures in Western society?

4. Which do you like better, Coke or Pepsi? Or do you prefer another brand?

United Nations Development Programme

Unit 10

©2001 United Nations—100 people (Gold Lion)

I. Preliminary Reading: *This section provides preliminary background information for the TV commercial you are going to watch and listen to. Read the passage carefully and do the tasks that follow.*

Planet Earth is human beings' only home. Thus, we need to share it, like a large family living in a small house without much space to spare. The family can only live happily together if they respect each other; if they do not—if any one member bullies another—happiness will never be theirs.

This simple illustration should serve as an excellent tip on how we can live in harmony here on this Earth of ours. Unfortunately, however, bullying still plagues human society in the form of conflicts and disputes among peoples of various nationalities, ethnic backgrounds, and religions.

Since prehistoric days, when human civilization first arose, people have been fighting against each other, mainly because civilization has made them greedy, demanding everything in more and more abundance. The economic gap between the rich and poor in society has often been the cause of conflicts, and human history has seen wars too numerous to count up until the present day.

The Earth is subject to natural disasters of all kinds, such as earthquakes, hurricanes, typhoons, tsunamis, volcanic eruptions, cyclones, and others. So why do we continue to waste our time killing each other and damaging the Earth's environment to the breaking point? The sooner we stop fighting each other in wars, the sooner the environment will regain its health. If a country has enough wealth to spare to conduct a war, it should instead direct that wealth to saving "Mother Earth."

It has always been assumed that human beings were the most intelligent species on this planet, but recent events have revealed that humans are the stupidest and most arrogant species of all because they are destroying their own irreplaceable home forever.

2. **Vocabulary Build-up:** *Find the highlighted words in the reading that match the following descriptions and write them in the parentheses, as in the example.*

   Example: An event causing great loss of life or damage (disaster)
   1. A hint or suggestion   (   )
   2. Very many   (   )
   3. An example   (   )
   4. Overly desirous or hungry   (   )
   5. To disclose or to make known   (   )

3. **Reading Comprehension:** *Choose the sentence below which most closely matches the content of the reading passage.*

   1. The Earth is just like a small house, so it is impossible for all the family members to live happily together.
   2. Human history has been marked by wasteful conflicts between the haves and the have-nots since human beings first formed their civilization.
   3. The wealthy countries should direct their wealth to fighting their enemies instead of trying to return the environment to good health.
   4. It has always been believed that human beings are the most arrogant and stupidest of all the species on this planet.

Tasks for the TV Commercial

4. **Vocabulary Preview:** *Here are some key words/phrases you need to know to understand the TV commercial for this lesson. Match each with a word/phrase of similar meaning in the box below.*

   1. consist of (   )   2. wealth (   )   3. cosmetics (   )   4. donation (   )
   5. weapon   (   )   6. means (   )   7. poverty   (   )

   ```
   a. way      b. being poor    c. make-up      d. gift
        e. property      f. gun      g. be composed of
   ```

5. **Soundtrack Listening:** *Listen to the soundtrack of the commercial without looking at the screen. Then number the words/phrases/sentences below in the order in which you hear them. You can replay the soundtrack as many times as you like. Two have been done for you as examples.*

   a. One hundred people   (1)   f. Ninety percent of the world's wealth (   )
   b. Eight would be African   (   )   g. The first generation   (   )
   c. Point two percent   (   )   h. One or more TVs   (   )
   d. Our basic education   (   )   i. One near death   (   )
   e. Spent on cosmetics   (   )   j. One of them   (10)

6. Story Line Completion: *There are 20 scenes in the TV commercial for this lesson, some of which are described on the chart below. Watch the video closely and then write brief descriptions of the missing scenes to complete the commercial's story line. Use the descriptions below as models.*

Scene 1	Scene 2	Scene 3	Scene 4	Scene 5
A football Stadium		A chef surrounded by vacationers	American tourists taking pictures of two African children	

Scene 6	Scene 7	Scene 8	Scene 9	Scene 10
A video of a baby in the womb	A dying baby			A starving African

Scene 11	Scene 12	Scene 13	Scene 14	Scene 15
Children pointing guns at the sky		A red sign reading "Danger! Mines!"	A man carrying a cardboard box for a TV	

Scene 16	Scene 17	Scene 18	Scene 19	Scene 20
A man smoking in a car	A woman covering her face with her handbag		A man walking with his girlfriend	

7. Transcript Completion: *As you watch and listen to the commercial again, fill in the blanks in the transcript below.*

1. If the world _____ people, _____ would _____, _____ would _____, six would _____, eight would _____, and _____ would _____.

2. One would be _____ and one _____. Twenty people would own _____. And while _____ is _____ than _____, fifteen people would _____. And because ten times more money _____ than on _____, sixteen people wouldn't _____.

3. Twenty people would have _____ TVs at home. Seventeen wouldn't _____. These twenty people are _____ that have _____ with only _____, and since you're _____ watching TV, _____ one of them.

8. Finding the Commercial's Message: *Choose the sentence which best expresses the main message of the commercial.*

1. The people watching this commercial are all comparatively wealthy and capable of helping the world's poor simply by donating only point two percent of their wealth.
2. The twenty percent of the world's population who own 90 percent of the world's wealth spend too much money on cosmetics and too much time watching TV.
3. More money should be spent on food donations and basic education because 20 percent of the first generation of TV viewers now have the means to end world poverty.

9. Utilizing Useful Words and Phrases: *Rearrange the words/phrases in parentheses below to make complete English sentences. Then translate the sentences into Japanese.*

1. (consists / wealthy / the world / just / of / a few / countries) and many poor countries.

   _____

2. If I had a million dollars, (over / the / I / all / world / would / travel).

   _____

3. My uncle (more money / has / twenty / my father / times / than).

4. The new (the means / President / to end / had / poverty) in the country.

5. (spent on / money / three / more / was / times) the construction of the bridge than was originally planned.

10. Optional Activity: *Read your completed transcript (from Task 7 above) aloud as you watch the commercial with the sound off. Match the words with the images.*

11. Topics for Discussion: *Discuss the following topics in class, or write a short paragraph expressing your ideas on each topic.*

1. How does the fact that only 20 percent of the world's population own 90 percent of the world's wealth make you feel?

2. Ten times more money is spent on weapons than on basic education. How does that make you feel?

3. What can we do as individuals to help eliminate poverty in the world?

4. What does UNDP stand for, and what is the organization's objective?

Unit 11

Disney—Magic Happens

1. Preliminary Reading:
This section provides preliminary background information for the TV commercial you are going to watch and listen to. Read the passage carefully and do the tasks that follow.

©2002 Disney (Silver Lion)

The **amusement** park on the outskirts of Tokyo known as Tokyo Disneyland attracts more than 16 million people a year. As everyone knows, the **prototype** for Tokyo Disneyland is the original Disneyland in Anaheim, California, which, as everyone also knows, was founded by Walt Disney, a great animated filmmaker as well as a successful
5 businessman.

Disney was **outstanding** in that he somehow turned children's culture into everybody's dream. The animated movies he produced were popular with adults as well as children. Every **cartoon** character he created—Mickey Mouse, Donald Duck, Goofy, and many others—was loved by children and adults all across the United States. By taking
10 stories from various countries and cultures, Disney successfully **introduced** them into American culture. Disney Productions has made movies retelling folk tales originating in Europe, Africa, America, the Middle East, Asia, and Australia, and has spread the Disney message around the world.

After succeeding in the film business, Walt Disney focused his talents and attention
15 on creating the world's biggest amusement park, where he **transformed** his fantasy movies and characters into real-life attractions. He wanted to make his "magic **kingdom** " a place where people from all continents could enjoy themselves **regardless** of age, nationality, race, or social status.

An amusement park is, naturally, isolated from the real world and all its social,
20 racial, and religious troubles and **conflicts**. The more problems there are in everyday life, the greater the number of people who are likely to want to **escape** these problems by visiting an amusement park. The magic kingdom can be a place where ordinary people can make their dreams come true by becoming a Cinderella or Prince Charming for a day.

2. **Vocabulary Build-up:** *Find the highlighted words in the reading that match the following descriptions and write them in the parentheses, as in the example.*

   Example: Fight or battle   (conflict   )
   1. To convert   (   )
   2. Excellent   (   )
   3. Original model   (   )
   4. To run away from   (   )
   5. To show or explain for the first time (   )

3. **Reading Comprehension:** *Choose the sentence below which most closely matches the content of the reading passage.*

   1. The prototype of Disneyland, which was founded by Walt Disney, is in Tokyo.
   2. The name Walt Disney became well known to children and adults all across the United States only after Disneyland opened.
   3. Walt Disney wanted to make his amusement park a place where children could enjoy themselves and be independent of their parents for a day.
   4. An amusement park like Disneyland is an isolated place where people can go to escape the troubles and conflicts of the outside world.

Tasks for the TV Commercial

4. **Vocabulary Preview:** *Here are some key words/phrases you need to know to understand the TV commercial for this lesson. Match each with a word/phrase of similar meaning in the box below.*

   1. occasion   (   )   2. get engaged   (   )   3. reduction   (   )
   4. shrink   (   )   5. anniversary   (   )   6. suspect   (   )

   > a. think   b. discount   c. grow smaller
   > d. promise to marry   e. event   f. yearly celebration

5. **Soundtrack Listening:** *Listen to the soundtrack of the commercial without looking at the screen. Then number the words/phrases/sentences below in the order in which you hear them. You can replay the soundtrack as many times as you like. Two have been done for you as examples.*

   a. What's the occasion?   (1)   f. I got you a little something. (   )
   b. No! Anything important.   (   )   g. Our anniversary   (   )
   c. I wasn't expecting shoes.   (   )   h. Can you believe it?   (   )
   d. Yeah, you know. Cathy.   (   )   i. Open it.   (   )
   e. Open the box, please.   (   )   j. He got me a shoe.   (10)

6. **Story Line Completion:** The sentences below describe the scenes in the commercial for this lesson. Watch the video and then complete the commercial's story line by numbering the sentences in the order in which the scenes appear.

   1. The woman asks the man if he remembers what day it is. ( )
   2. The man hands the woman a box. ( )
   3. The man wonders what the dish called "Filet Reduction" is. ( )
   4. The man urges the woman to open the box. ( )
   5. A couple are sitting at a table in a fancy restaurant. ( )
   6. The woman is disappointed when she first sees the box. ( )
   7. They are talking about their mutual friend Cathy. ( )
   8. The woman opens the box and finds a glass slipper in it. ( )

7. **Scene Description:** Watch the commercial again and answer the following questions.

   1. Describe the man's physical features and clothing.

   2. Describe the woman's physical features and clothing.

   3. Describe what the man gives to his girlfriend.

   4. What do you think the elderly woman says to her husband?

8. **Transcript Completion:** As you watch and listen to the commercial again, fill in the blanks in the transcript below.

Woman:	So, this place is nice. What's the occasion?
Man:	Oh, _____ .
Woman:	_____ .
Man:	Thanks.
Woman:	Oh, _____ .
Man:	Cathy?
Woman:	Yeah, _____ . Cathy.
Man:	Great, yeah, Cathy. _____ ?
Woman:	Well, she and Dan finally _____ .
Man:	Oh.
Woman:	_____ ?
Man:	_____ . I mean they've been going out _____ .
Woman:	Yeah.

Man: What's a Filet Reduction? Is that a small steak?
Woman: So my dad said that you called him?
Man: Right. _____?
Woman: No! _____?
Man: Yeah. I wanted to see if he could tape _____.
Woman: Oh.
Man: _____ that shrinks when you cook it.
Woman: (Sigh) _____ what _____?
Man: Today?
Woman: Our _____. The day _____.
Man: Oh, right, yeah! Oh. Of course, I know what today is. _____, I got you _____.
Woman: You did?
Man: Yeah. I was hoping it would _____.
Woman: Oh, it is. I never suspected you'd . . . _____ . . . _____.
Man: _____. Open it.
Woman: _____.
Man: _____.
Woman: No, it's not that, it's just . . . _____.
Man: Lisa, _____ . . . please. I, . . . I think I'm supposed to help you put that on.
Woman: Uh huh.
Man: Perfect fit.
Woman: _____.

9. **Utilizing Useful Words and Phrases:** *Rearrange the words/phrases in parentheses below to make complete English sentences. Then translate the sentences into Japanese.*

1. (your / up / dad / to / what's)?

2. John and Mary (been / a / long / have / going out / time / for).

3. (you / to see / I / wanted / could / if) do the honors for me.

4. I was (would / hoping / a surprise / it / be).

5. (to help / you / I'm / complete / supposed) the project report.

10. Optional Activity: *Read your completed transcript (from Task 8 above) aloud as you watch the commercial with the sound off. Match the words with the action.*

11. Topics for Discussion: *Discuss the following topics in class, or write a short paragraph expressing your ideas on each topic.*

1. What answer does the woman expect from her boyfriend when she says, "Anything . . . important?"

2. What does Lisa assume the glass shoe means?

3. What does the man mean by giving a glass slipper to his girlfriend?

Coca-Cola—For Everyone

Unit 12

1. Preliminary Reading: This section provides preliminary background information for the TV commercial you are going to watch and listen to. Read the passage carefully and do the tasks that follow.

©2002 Coca-Cola (Silver Lion)

When traveling alone in a foreign country, with no guides, no acquaintances, and no friends to help you, who would you ask how to buy a ticket, or how to get to the right platform to take the right train, or how to take a taxi to your hotel? Don't worry. All you have to do is follow the signs posted on walls or hanging from ceilings and you will not lose your way. This is just one example of how important signs are in our daily lives.

Signs often use simplified symbols so that they can be easily understood by ordinary people, including complete strangers to the place, or by people who do not read or understand the local language. A simplified picture of a train indicates where to catch your train; a simple suitcase shows you where to pick up your luggage.

Traffic signs are another good example of the use of simplified pictures. When you see a yellow sign with the silhouette of a child walking painted on it, you know you should drive slowly because a child or children might be crossing the street. A picture of a deer warns the driver to drive carefully because an animal may jump out onto the road. You will see many other examples when you travel abroad, and you will probably notice that most of the signs are either very similar or exactly the same in most countries.

Ideally, these signs with simplified pictures, or symbols, should be common to all countries. They should not be decided at random. Certain rules must be applied internationally or, otherwise, the signs will not help but only confuse people. These signs or symbols are designed to make life easier for all of us no matter where we are and what language we speak.

2. Vocabulary Build-up: Find the highlighted words in the reading that match the following descriptions and write them in the parentheses, as in the example.

Example: To make something less clear (*confuse*)
1. A person whom one knows ( )
2. Bags and suitcases ( )
3. A person whom one does not know ( )
4. To show or state something ( )
5. A dark outline of something ( )

3. Reading Comprehension: Choose the sentence below which most closely matches the content of the reading passage.

1. When visiting an unfamiliar place, you do not have to worry because simplified signs will help you.
2. Complicated symbols should not be used because they too obviously attract people's attention.
3. When you are traveling abroad, you will find that each country has its own system of traffic signals and signs.
4. Signs and symbols often confuse travelers because there are no international rules governing them.

Tasks for the TV Commercial

4. Vocabulary Preview: Here are some key words you need to know to understand the TV commercial for this lesson. Match each with a word/phrase of similar meaning in the box below.

1. castaway ( ) 2. pessimistic ( ) 3. optimistic ( ) 4. cautious ( )
5. skinny ( ) 6. astronaut ( ) 7. transparent ( ) 8. anxious ( )

> a. person trained for space flight   b. see-through   c. cheerful
> d. very thin   e. uneasy and worried   f. survivor of a shipwreck
> g. negative about the future   h. careful

5. Soundtrack Listening: Listen to the soundtrack of the commercial without looking at the screen. Then number the words/phrases/sentences below in the order in which you hear them. You can replay the soundtrack as many times as you like. Two have been done for you as examples.

a. For the tall (1)   f. For the near sighted ( )
b. For those who live together ( )   g. For the ones who participate ( )
c. For everyone ( )   h. For kissers ( )
d. For the well-mannered ( )   i. For those who have nothing ( )
e. For those who love you a lot ( )   j. For those who write (6)

6. Scene Description: *Watch the commercial and answer the following questions.*

1. How would you describe the symbol for "for those that laugh"?

   _____

2. What is the symbol for "for the anxious"?

   _____

3. How would you describe the symbol for "for the well-mannered"?

   _____

4. What is the symbol for "for nudists"?

   _____

5. How would you describe the symbol for "for kissers"?

   _____

7. Transcript Completion: *As you watch and listen to the commercial again, fill in the blanks in the partial transcript below.*

1. For the fat, for _____, for the tall, for _____, for those that laugh, for _____, for those who cry, for _____, for the pessimistic, for those who have it all, for _____.

2. For _____, for the players, for _____, for the families, for _____, for kings, for _____, for the committed.

3. For _____, for those who love you, for _____, for those who love you a little, for _____.

4. For _____, for twins, for _____, for clowns, for _____, for those who live together.

5. For men, for _____, for her, for _____, for the transparent, for _____, for the ones who excel, for _____.

8. Finding the Commercial's Message: *Choose the sentence which does NOT express the main message of the TV commercial.*

1. Coca-Cola can be drunk by anyone, anytime, anywhere.
2. Coca-Cola is the perfect drink for every occasion.
3. Coca-Cola is not to everyone's taste.

9. **Utilizing Useful Words and Phrases:** *Rearrange the words/phrases in parentheses below to make complete English sentences. Then translate the sentences into Japanese.*

   1. (take / should / of / the strong / care / the weak).

   2. (only to / is / opportunity /offered / this / truly committed / the).

   3. The government (this action / who / taking / is / live alone / to help / those).

   4. (have it all / between / and / those who / the gap / those who / have nothing) is getting wider.

10. **Optional Activity:** *Read your completed transcript (from Task 7 above) aloud as you watch the commercial with the sound off. Match the words with the images.*

11. **Topics for Discussion:** *Discuss the following topics in class, or write a short paragraph expressing your ideas on each topic.*

    1. Have you ever played, "He loves me, he loves me not"?

    2. Pick out several symbols in the Coca-Cola commercial and explain them. (Some of the symbols are already discussed in Task 6 above: "for those that laugh," "for the anxious," "for the well-mannered," "for nudists," and "for kissers.")

Anti-Smoking Campaign

Unit 13

©2005 Fair Enough (Bronze Lion)

1. Preliminary Reading: This section provides preliminary background information for the TV commercials you are going to watch and listen to. Read the passage carefully and do the tasks that follow.

When the first Spanish explorers and the members of their crew landed in what they called the New World, they saw the natives burning dried leaves and inhaling the smoke. This strange practice was brought back to the explorers' homeland, from where it soon spread to other European countries, to the Middle East, and to the Far East.

Among Native Americans, smoking tobacco and inhaling the nicotine it contained was used as a form of physical and mental medication, though smoking also had important social and ritual connotations. The reason smoking spread all over the world so quickly was because of its pleasurable relaxation effect. Eventually, smoking tobacco came to be seen as a sophisticated habit. Actors and actresses were seen smoking cigarettes in many old movies, which added to tobacco's mystique. As a result, smoking was regarded as fashionable and cool, especially among young people.

Although smoking was very popular, it was not long before people began to be concerned about its negative effects on the health. Even as early as the beginning of the 20th century, many smokers began to realize that excessive smoking would harm their health. In the 1950s, scientists published research data suggesting a close link between tobacco smoking and lung cancer.

Today, many national and local governments strictly prohibit smoking in public places. Anti-smoking campaigns warn that nicotine is addictive, increases blood sugar, disturbs metabolism, and causes heart disease, cancer, and many other physical ailments. Smoking is no longer seen as an appropriate dramatic expression in movies and TV shows.

According to the 2002 WHO report on tobacco smoking, about 36% of the population of China, 35% of Korea, 19% of Sweden, 24% of the USA, and 33% of Japan still smoked. These numbers should drop dramatically in the coming years as more and more smokers become aware that they could get very sick or even die as a result of their habit.

2. **Vocabulary Build-up:** Find the highlighted words in the reading that match the following descriptions and write them in the parentheses, as in the example.

   Example: To find fault with (criticize)
   1. To breathe in ( )
   2. Treatment or cure ( )
   3. Unfavorable ( )
   4. To become aware of ( )
   5. The total number of inhabitants of a town, city, country, etc. ( )

3. **Reading Comprehension:** Choose the sentence below which most closely matches the content of the reading passage.

   1. Native Americans brought the practice of burning dried tobacco leaves and inhaling the smoke to Europe, the Middle East, and the Far East.
   2. Native Americans saw smoking tobacco as fashionable, so there were many scenes showing Native Americans smoking in many old Western movies.
   3. Smoking scenes in movies and TV dramas are prohibited because tobacco increases the actors' blood sugar, as well as causes heart disease and many other physical problems.
   4. According to the 2002 report on smoking by WHO, many people around the world still smoke, though this should change as we learn more about the harmful effects of smoking.

Tasks for TV Commercials No. 1 and No. 2

4. **Vocabulary Preview:** Here are some key words you need to know to understand the TV commercials for this lesson. Match each with a word/phrase of similar meaning in the box below.

   1. considering ( )   2. episode ( )   3. decal ( )
   4. subliminal ( )   5. logo ( )   6. carton ( )

   | a. box | b. trademark | c. seal | d. story | e. unconscious | f. judging from |

5. **Soundtrack Listening:** Listen to the soundtracks of TV Commercials No. 1 and No. 2 without looking at the screen. Then number the words/phrases/sentences below in the order in which you hear them. You can replay the soundtracks as many times as you like. Two have been done for you as examples.

   TV Commercial No. 1
   a. Marie (1)
   b. Seven years old ( )
   c. In the bedroom ( )
   d. 22,430 ( )
   e. 18,930 ( )
   f. In the living room ( )
   g. In the dining room ( )

   TV Commercial No. 2
   a. Our cigarette packs (4)
   b. Sir ( )
   c. Logo oriented ( )
   d. This episode ( )
   e. The family boat ( )
   f. The complete series ( )
   g. The carton ( )

6. Scene Description: *Watch TV Commercial No. 1 and answer the following questions.*

TV Commercial No. 1

1. Where is the man standing?

2. Is there anyone in the dining room?

3. What is in the glass tank in addition to cigarette butts?

4. What is on the desk in the bedroom?

5. What is the little girl doing?

7. Story Line Completion: *The sentences below describe the scenes in Commercial No. 2. Watch the video and then complete the commercial's story line by numbering the sentences in the order in which the scenes appear.*

TV Commercial No. 2
1. The two senior executives pretend to like the junior office worker's idea. ( )
2. The junior office worker starts to present his promotion plan. ( )
3. Two senior executives are talking in an office. ( )
4. The story takes place in a tall office building. ( )
5. A junior staff member shows up at the doorway of the office. ( )

8. Transcript Completion: *As you watch and listen to the commercials again, fill in the blanks in the transcripts below.*

TV Commercial No. 1

Since Marie has _____, she has smoked _____ _____ in the living room, 22,430 _____, _____ in the dining room, 18,930 _____, _____ in the bedroom. _____, Marie has smoked _____. That's a lot, _____.

TV Commercial No. 2

1. This _____ a 1989 Big Tobacco _____.
2. Sir, _____ are very decal _____ and logo _____.
3. So _____ decals with subliminal _____.
4. Our younger smokers might _____, purses . . .
5. We develop _____ and _____ the complete series.
6. Buy _____.

Unit 13

9. **Utilizing Useful Words and Phrases:** *Rearrange the words/phrases in parentheses below to make complete English sentences. Then translate the sentences into Japanese.*

   1. (on / based / his novel / experiences / is / his real) during the war.

   2. Today's (are / Japanese / conscious/ very / youth / harmony) and group-oriented.

   3. (the promotion / start / what / we / campaign/ if) without our boss's permission?

   4. (don't / place / on / why / you / a "No Junk Mail" sticker) your mailbox?

10. **Optional Activity:** *Read your completed transcript (from Task 8 above) aloud as you watch the commercial with the sound off. Match the word with the action.*

11. **Topics for Discussion:** *Discuss the following topics in class, or write a short paragraph expressing your ideas on each topic.*

    1. Discuss why you smoke or why you do not smoke.

    2. Do you think all public places should be strictly smoke free?

    3. Do you know anyone who has or has had a disease caused by smoking?

Counterfeit Mini Coopers

Unit 14

©2005 Mini Cooper (Gold Lion) UNTERFEITMINI.ORG

1. Preliminary Reading: *This section provides preliminary background information for the TV commercial you are going to watch and listen to. Read the passage carefully and do the tasks that follow.*

The most valuable talent human beings possess is the ability to create things, a talent which separates humans from most other animals. The history of human beings is full of wonderful creations, such as literature, music, paintings and sculptures, and so on. No one really knows who originally started communicating by telling and writing stories or by composing melodies, but literature and music have been created and handed down for the benefit of others for centuries and centuries. This accumulation of cultural wealth forms a valuable part of any nation's social heritage.

To create or invent something which has never before existed often requires time, energy, and money. For example, it usually takes years to complete a novel, a lot of energy to compose a symphony, and millions of dollars to produce a Hollywood movie. Copying these works of art, however, is a much easier process. Today, almost anyone can do it. In order to protect the authors and creators of the originals, a system of reward needs to be established to enable the original artists to benefit from all copies produced.

Most people respect an artist's rights and understand that the efforts of the creator should be protected. But unfortunately, there are always some people who ignore these rights and copy or sell duplicated products or counterfeits, thereby making huge illegal profits. For this reason, laws relating to copyright and trademarks have been established for the protection of authors, composers, artists, manufacturers, and producers.

Copyright is a form of protection provided to the creators of original works such as books, computer software, songs, designs, and other unique ideas. Trademarks are a form of recognition of the names or symbols which signify the originality of the products and distinguish them from other similar products. Trademarks are always found on such products—bags, clothing, accessories, and many other consumer items—to inform shoppers that they are getting the real thing.

2. Vocabulary Build-up: Find the highlighted words in the reading that match the following descriptions and write them in the parentheses, as in the example.

Example: To make something new (*invent*)
1. Anything handed down from the past ( )
2. To make a copy of ( )
3. Benefit or payment ( )
4. To neglect or pay no attention to ( )
5. To show a difference ( )

3. Reading Comprehension: Choose the sentence below which most closely matches the content of the reading passage.

1. Today, humans beings' unique ability to produce and hand down their creations and inventions needs to be protected since it has become very easy to copy those creations.
2. Copying such works of art as a symphony, a novel, or a movie costs producers millions of dollars.
3. Today, almost anyone has the time, talent, and money to create wonderful works of art such as novels, movies, and symphonies.
4. Copyright protects the rights of the producers of copied works and trademarks provide protection to the manufacturers of copied products.

Tasks for the TV Commercial

4. Vocabulary Preview: Here are some key words you need to know to understand the TV commercial for this lesson. Match each with a word of similar meaning in the box below.

1. merchandise ( )   2. genuine ( )   3. premium ( )   4. fool ( )
5. counterfeit ( )   6. bucks ( )   7. humiliate ( )

> a. superior   b. authentic   c. imitation   d. trick
> e. embarrass   f. products   g. dollars

5. Soundtrack Listening: Listen to the soundtrack of the TV commercial without looking at the screen. Then number the words/phrases/sentences below in the order in which you hear them. You can replay the soundtrack as many times as you like. Two have been done for you as examples.

a. Around the globe (1)   f. Mini's signature look ( )
b. Until they tried ( )   g. Counterfeit brand-name merchandise ( )
c. Wrong ( )   h. Your Mini is genuine ( )
d. That's why ( )   i. Humiliated victims ( )
e. Don't be fooled ( )   j. Visit counterfeitmini.org (10)

6. **Story Line Completion:** *The sentences below describe the scenes in the commercial. Watch the video and then complete the commercial's story line by numbering the sentences in the order in which the scenes appear.*

   1. A genuine Mini Cooper turns a corner easily, but the others cannot. ( )
   2. There are six Mini-featured cars but only one genuine Mini Cooper. ( )
   3. The announcer announces that a DVD of counterfeit Mini Coopers is available now from CCC. ( )
   4. Some body shop workers are painting small cars to make them look like Mini Coopers. ( )
   5. Counterfeit watches and sunglasses are being sold in a crowded street. ( )
   6. A man says he bought a fake Mini for 1,200 bucks. ( )
   7. A white-gloved hand reveals the genuine Mini emblem. ( )

7. **Scene Description:** *Watch the commercial again and answer the following questions.*

   1. What are the brand names of the counterfeit watches, bags, and sunglasses shown in the commercial?

   2. What organization issues the DVD about counterfeit Mini Coopers?

   3. What are the body shop workers doing in the counterfeit factory?

   4. When can you tell the difference between a genuine Mini and a fake?

   5. How much does the "Counterfeit Mini Coopers" DVD cost?

8. **Transcript Completion:** *As you watch and listen to the commercial again, fill in the blanks in the transcript below.*

   1. It's happening _____.
   2. People getting _____; _____.
   3. You _____ what else is _____.
   4. That's why _____ the Counter Counterfeit Commission.
   5. You'll get a crash course on _____.
   6. We'll even take you overseas and _____ Mini's signature look.
   7. No one can tell _____ until _____.
   8. Don't _____.
   9. Be _____ your Mini _____.
   10. _____ "Counterfeit Mini Coopers" _____ <counterfeitmini.org>.

Unit 14

9. **Utilizing Useful Words and Phrases:** *Rearrange the words/phrases in parentheses below to make complete English sentences. Then translate the sentences into Japanese.*

   1. (take / we / that's / every / should / why / kind) of action to prevent global warming.

   2. (certain / the doors / be / locked / all / are) before you leave.

   3. Customers at the bag store (imitations / were / by / fooled / brand-name).

   4. (one / until / can / the difference / no / tell) they have tried many kinds of good and bad wines.

10. **Optional Activity:** *Read your completed transcript (from Task 8 above) aloud as you watch the commercial with the sound off. Match the words with the action.*

11. **Topics for Discussion:** *Discuss the following topics in class, or write a short paragraph expressing your ideas on each topic.*

    1. Some people say that trademarks, copyrights, and patents are too strictly protected by law. What do you think?

    2. What kind of illegal counterfeit goods are most often seen in Japan?

    3. What does the gesture (known as "air quotes") of raising two hands and simultaneously wiggling the index and middle fingers of both hands mean?

Unit 15

Hallmark of a Teacher

©2002 Hallmark (Bronze Lion)

I. Preliminary Reading: *This section provides preliminary background information for the TV commercial you are going to watch and listen to. Read the passage carefully and do the tasks that follow.*

The girl was born in the U.S. state of Alabama in 1880. When she was two, she suffered from a high fever and lost her sight and hearing. She was not able to communicate with her parents, nor did they know how to deal with her. All they did was to give her whatever she wanted. As a result, she became rough, spoilt, and wild —like an animal. Her parents needed help to raise her and so they hired a tutor, who was also visually disabled. The tutor accomplished a miracle. She taught the girl how to communicate with others and how to study and learn. And she taught her how to behave like a human being.

In the end, the girl managed to overcome her disability and even graduated from college. She then traveled around the world and devoted her life to assisting physically disabled people and eliminating discrimination against them. She passed away in 1968 and was buried together with her lifetime friend and teacher in Washington National Cathedral on the outskirts of Washington, D.C. The girl was, of course, Helen Keller, and her teacher was Annie Sullivan. Without Annie Sullivan's assistance, Helen would never have been able to achieve her true dignity as a human being. Annie Sullivan's first success in communicating with Helen Keller as a child became the basis of an immortal theatrical work and, later, a movie entitled *The Miracle Worker*.

Annie Sullivan is still esteemed by many as an example of what the ideal teacher should be because of her strong desire and will to guide her student along the right path in life. A teacher is a professional who greatly influences the minds of members of the next generation, and, in giving them lifelong goals and learning tools, is regarded by his/her students as a role model. Like a farmer, a teacher is a dedicated worker who plants and raises seeds, helping them to bloom and to grow up to be a beautiful addition to the world.

2. **Vocabulary Build-up:** Find the highlighted words in the reading that match the following descriptions and write them in the parentheses, as in the example.

   Example: Suburbs   (outskirts   )
   1. The quality of self-respect   (   )
   2. To feel pain in body or mind   (   )
   3. A private teacher   (   )
   4. Prejudice   (   )
   5. To defeat   (   )

3. **Reading Comprehension:** Choose the sentence below which most closely matches the content of the reading passage.

   1. Soon after Helen was born in the state of Alabama, she became seriously ill, but fortunately her parents knew how to handle her.
   2. Miss Sullivan was a doctor who cured Helen's sight and hearing disabilities, and showed her how to live as a healthy human being.
   3. A teacher is a person who brings out the best in his/her pupils, and Annie Sullivan was an ideal example of such a teacher.
   4. Annie Sullivan is still respected as an ideal farmer because she planted seeds, raised them, and helped them to bloom.

Tasks for the TV Commercial

4. **Vocabulary Preview:** Here are some key words you need to know to understand the TV commercial for this lesson. Match each with a word/phrase of similar meaning in the box below.

   1. apology (   )   2. ruin   (   )   3. retire (   )   4. physician (   )
   5. bloom   (   )   6. investment (   )   7. guru   (   )

   > a. putting money into a company   b. leader   c. doctor   d. destroy
   > e. have flowers   f. regret   g. leave one's job

5. Soundtrack Listening (1): *Listen to the soundtrack of the commercial without looking at the screen. Then number the words/phrases/sentences below in the order in which you hear them. You can replay the soundtrack as many times as you like. Two have been done for you as examples.*

a. Professor Foley (1)
b. I'll never find my glasses ( )
c. A while ago ( )
d. You may not remember all the things ( )
e. You were retiring ( )
f. Beth Hooper ( )
g. Birth Order and Early Childhood Development ( )
h. My apologies ( )
i. Bonsai trees ( )
j. Investment banker (10)

6. Soundtrack Listening (2): *Listen to the soundtrack again and put the words/phrases in parentheses below into the correct order.*

1. Hooper, (you / Bonsai trees / where / on / do / stand)?

2. Of course, (be / my father / a physician / always / wanted / me / to).

3. You may (remember / you've / all / not / the / that / done / things).

4. Everywhere around you (are / and / growing / blooming / are / seeds / people).

7. Scene Description: *Watch the commercial and answer the following questions.*

1. Where does the action of the commercial take place?

2. What do you think Professor Foley is doing?

3. What made Beth Hooper come by the professor's office?

4. Describe Professor Foley and what he is wearing.

5. What does the professor do after he hears that Beth became a teacher?

Unit 15

8. **Transcript Completion:** As you watch and listen to the commercial again, fill in the blanks in the transcript below.

Beth: Professor Foley?
Professor: Yes.
Beth: You wouldn't _____. My name is Beth Hooper. I was _____, uh, _____.
Professor: My apologies. I hope I didn't _____.
Beth: No. No, in fact I always _____ and tell you . . . well I, I, I heard _____, so I . . .
Professor: Hooper, _____ Bonsai trees?
Beth: Bonsai trees?
Professor: _____ I might start raising Bonsai trees now.
Beth: Oh! Well, anyway, I just came by to, to _____.
Professor: Of course, _____ to be a physician. I'll _____ in all of this. I'm afraid you're gonna have to _____.
Beth: Who in their life hasn't planted a seed just hoping that _____ would grow? _____ all the things that you've done, but _____ seeds are growing and people are blooming. _____, I'm _____.
Professor: "Birth Order and Early Childhood Development."
Beth: That's right! That was . . . That was me. That was _____.
Professor: _____, Hooper. Thank you. So, Hooper, _____? Investment banker? Internet guru?
Beth: No. _____.

9. **Utilizing Useful Words and Phrases:** Rearrange the words/phrases in parentheses below to make complete English sentences. Then translate the sentences into Japanese.

1. (you / where / on / do / this issue / stand)?

2. The manager (to do / asked / by welcoming / the honors / his secretary) the overseas guests for him.

3. The teacher asked the pupil, "(you / what / do / want to / when you / be) grow up?"

_____

_____

4. When I arrived at the station, the stationmaster said, "(while / left / the train / for Osaka / a / ago)."

_____

_____

10. Optional Activity: *Read your completed transcript (from Task 8 above) aloud as you watch the commercial with the sound off. Match the words with the action.*

11. Topics for Discussion: *Discuss the following topics in class, or write a short paragraph expressing your ideas on each topic.*

1. Why did Professor Foley say, "My apologies. I hope I didn't ruin your entire life"?

_____

_____

2. What does the metaphor "seeds are growing and people are blooming" mean?

_____

_____

3. Why did Beth choose to become a teacher?

_____

_____

著作権法上、無断複写・複製は禁じられています。

English in 30 Seconds [B-618]
Award-Winning TV Commercials from Cannes Lions
[カンヌ国際広告祭受賞] TVコマーシャルで学ぶ異文化の世界

1　刷	2009年2月23日
18　刷	2024年3月29日

編著者　青木　雅幸　　Masayuki Aoki

発行者　南雲　一範　　Kazunori Nagumo
発行所　株式会社　南雲堂
　　　　〒162-0801　東京都新宿区山吹町361
　　　　NAN'UN-DO Publishing Co., Ltd.
　　　　361 Yamabuki-cho, Shinjuku-ku, Tokyo 162-0801, Japan
　　　　振替口座：00160-0-46863
　　　　TEL: 03-3268-2311（代表）／FAX: 03-3269-2486
　　　　編集者　TA/YS

製　版　スエナガ ヨウコ
印刷所　木元省美堂
装　丁　Nスタジオ
検　印　省　略
コード　ISBN 978-4-523-17618-3　C0082

Printed in Japan

E-mail　nanundo@post.email.ne.jp
URL　　https://www.nanun-do.co.jp